T0064666

Left Field . . .
In Glorious Toonarama

Left Field . . .
In Glorious Toonarama

The Delirious Cartoon Collection

Randy Halford

authorHOUSE®

AuthorHouse™ LLC
1663 Liberty Drive
Bloomington, IN 47403
www.authorhouse.com
Phone: 1-800-839-8640

© 2013 Randy Halford. All rights reserved.

No part of this book may be reproduced, stored in a retrieval system, or transmitted
by any means without the written permission of the author.

Published by AuthorHouse   11/15/2013

ISBN: 978-1-4918-1740-7 (sc)
ISBN: 978-1-4918-1739-1 (e)

Library of Congress Control Number: 2013920578

Any people depicted in stock imagery provided by Thinkstock are models,
and such images are being used for illustrative purposes only.
Certain stock imagery © Thinkstock.

This book is printed on acid-free paper.

Because of the dynamic nature of the Internet, any web addresses or links contained in this book may have changed
since publication and may no longer be valid. The views expressed in this work are solely those of the author and do
not necessarily reflect the views of the publisher, and the publisher hereby disclaims any responsibility for them.

FOREWARD

Not long ago, I clicked
my heels together three times (not as
dazzling in sneakers) and was magically transported
by twister from Idaho and plopped back
down in my old stomping grounds of
California. It's been quite an adjustment. The
good news is, I'm much closer to my family
again.
And that twister has given me quite a ride
as well on creativity. *Left Field* has been
the franchise that just refuses to die. Hence,
this is my fifth book...and there's *still* more
to come! I'm grateful that the well hasn't
run dry yet; just when I think I'm done, the
ideas come flooding back.
My cartoons have proven that a gay man like myself
can be as creatively warped as any straight man.
Words of wisdom? Don't allow narrow-minded people
to undermine your honesty, worth, confidence or stifle your
talent.
Be out. Be proud. Be you.
And finally, thanks again to Authorhouse for helping me
clear the hurdles a fifth time.
.Enough said. Enjoy the book!
Yours truly,

FOWL GAMES

THE Pig Pen PLEX

now playing:
"HOG DAY AFTERNOON"

coming soon:

"THE PIG SLEEP"
"THE TRUFFLE with ANGELS"
"THE APPRENTICESHIP of MUDDY
KRAVITZ"
"THE SEVENTH SQUEAL"
"THE HOGFATHER"
"GROSS OINK BLANK"
"HARRY POTTER AND THE PIG STY of
AZKABAN"
"GOSFORD PORK"
"SNORT AT THE DEVIL"
"THE FABULOUS BACON BOYS"
"MONTY PIGLET AND THE HOGLY GRAIL"
"ROBIN HOOF: PIG of THIEVES"
"OINK BREAK"

© 2010 Randy Cy

PIG PICTURES

BATMAN'S PUBLICIST

5

SHARK AUDITIONS

9

Mane MOVIEHOUSE

now playing:

"FROM HAIR to ETERNITY"

coming soon:

"AFRO-AMERICAN GRAFFITI"
"CURLYTOP GUN"
"AUNTIE MANE"
"THE PICTURE of POMPADOUR-IAN GRAY"
"LEGENDS of the FOLLICLE"
"FUNNY CURL"
"THE BEARD of LIVING DANGEROUSLY"
"BOUFFANT the VAMPIRE SLAYER"
"LAST of the MOHAWK-ANS"
"THE UNSINKABLE MULLET BROWN"
"HAIRY POTTER and the HALF-BUZZ CUT PRINCE"
"MUSTACHE ADO ABOUT NOTHING"
"A PONYTAIL of TWO CITIES"
"PERMS of ENDEARMENT"

HAIR FLICKS

SPEED DATING

12

CAT BURGLARS

13

THE SCI-FI CLASSIC "THEY CAME FROM PLANET CARBONATION"

14

SPIDER-MAN MEETS HIS DEADLIEST FOES YET

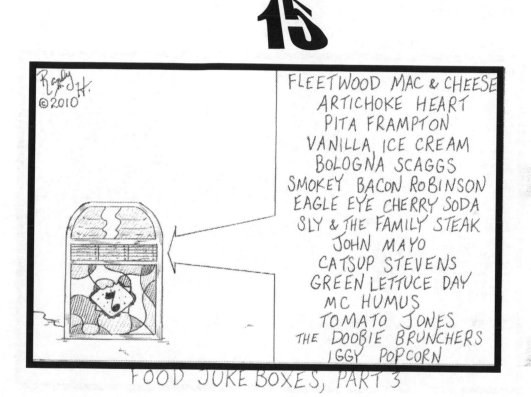

FLEETWOOD MAC & CHEESE
ARTICHOKE HEART
PITA FRAMPTON
VANILLA ICE CREAM
BOLOGNA SCAGGS
SMOKEY BACON ROBINSON
EAGLE EYE CHERRY SODA
SLY & THE FAMILY STEAK
JOHN MAYO
CATSUP STEVENS
GREEN LETTUCE DAY
MC HUMUS
TOMATO JONES
THE DOOBIE BRUNCHERS
IGGY POPCORN

FOOD JUKE BOXES, PART 3

16

17

FRUIT FLIES

18

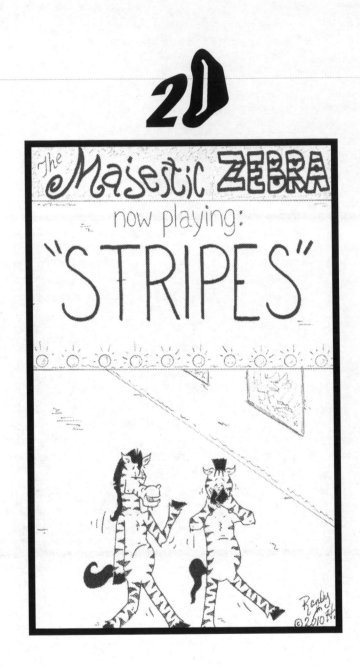

HORROR TELEVISION

22

IT SOON BECAME APPARENT TO AMY THAT SHE MIGHT BE SUFFERING FROM BIPOLAR DISORDER...

23

FRANK SPOONATRA

BOTTOM T.V. SCREEN PROMOS WE'D LIKE TO SEE BUT WON'T

FANTASY FOOTBALL SESSIONS

LOBSTER HAUNTED HOUSES

28

RAPPER FLAVOR FLAV AND HIS GRANDFATHER

DOG MOVIES

31

"WHO WANTS TO RIDE SHOTGUN?"

32

THE GUYS PLAYED THEIR BEST HANDS. STILL, NONE COULD PENETRATE STAN'S SEEMINGLY INVINCIBLE "POKER" FACE...

33

AGING GRACEFULLY

"RETURN OF THE JEDI: DA GANGSTA EDITION"

SODA BLIND DATES

"MY FAIR LADYBUG"

"A MIDSUMMER NIGHTCRAWLER'S DREAM"

"PEST SIDE STORY"

"KISS ME KATYDID"

"MANTIS of LaMANCHA"

©2010 Randy

BUG BROADWAY

GOD SMITES WITH THE "MAUDE" BUTTON

38

IMAGINE

DOG DISCUSSION FORUMS

WHEN CHAMELEONS PAINT

41

ELVIS PRIESTLEY
BILL HOLY AND THE COMETS
OZZY OSBOURNE-AGAIN
EDDIE RABBI
JUDAS CATHOLIC PRIEST
SACRED MADONNA
CHRISTIANITY AGUILERA
ORDAINED FAITH HILL
LUTHERAN VANDROSS
E-VAN-GELIST MORRISON
GOSPEL LIGHTFOOT
MOTLEY PEW
THE PRAY-TENDERS
ORCHESTRAL CONFESSIONS IN THE DARK
FROCK ZAPPA

RELIGIOUS JUKE BOXES

42

IF YOU CAN'T STAND THE HEAT...

43

"SWEET RIDE!"

44

46

SARCASTIC SPORTS SCORES

FUNNY FLICKS, PART 2

48

FLY IRONY

WHEN CAPTAIN AMERICA THROWS HIS MIGHTY SHIELD

52

BOTTOM T.V. SCREEN PROMOS WE'D
LIKE TO SEE BUT WON'T, PART 2

55

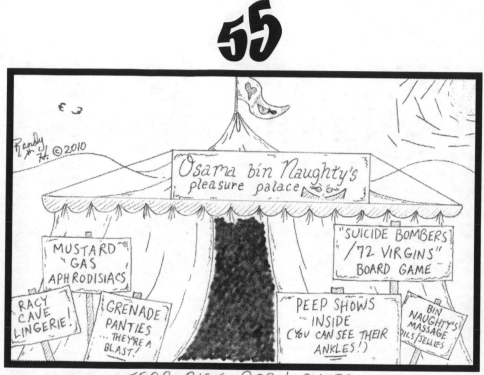

TERRORIST PORN SHOPS

56

DR. THICKHEAD, THE MOST CLUELESS JAMES BOND VILLAIN

PIPE DREAMS

58

ROACH MOTELS

"THAT WASN'T ANYTHING LIKE THE TITLE!"

RUBBER ASPHALT

DR. THICKHEAD, THE MOST CLUELESS JAMES BOND VILLAIN, PART 2

64

THE GAME SHOW "TASTES LIKE CHICKEN"

65

GEORGE THOROUGHBRED
HOOFIE AND THE BLOWFISH
JENNIFER GALLOPEZ
MICHAEL COLTON
HALL AND OAT FEED
MAROON MUSTANG 5
GREEN HAY
BRUCE SPRINGSTALLION
PONY BRAXTON
FODDER MC
RADIOHORSE
WHINNY NELSON
SADDLE McLACHLAN
DAVE MATTHEWS BARN
HORSESHOENIA TWAIN

HORSE JUKE BOXES

66

TRUTH-IN-ADVERTISING HORROR FLICKS

BUFFALO WINGS

68

CLAM THOUGHTS

69

CRAYON BARS

11

72

T.V.'s "ANIMAL ENTOURAGE"

73

74

THE "BATMAN" T.V. SHOW WITH GUEST VILLAIN STEVE MARTIN

SKUNK TELEVISION

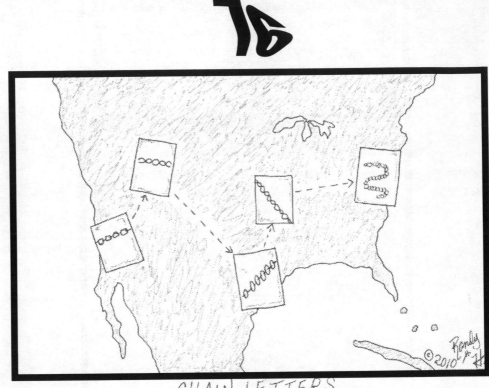

CHAIN LETTERS

77

78

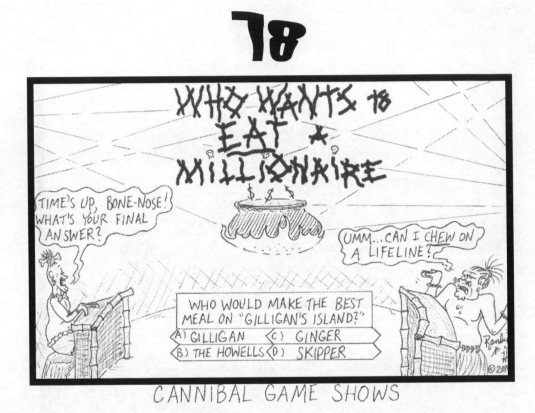

CANNIBAL GAME SHOWS

INDECISIVE MOVIES

80

THE DAZZLING LIVE SHOE SHOW "CIRQUE du SOLE"

81

83

MORON COWBOYS

83

84

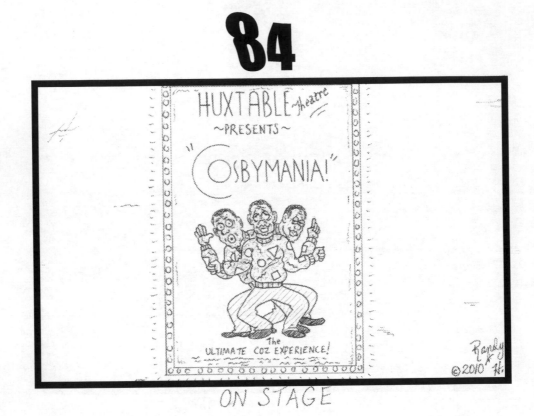

ON STAGE

85

T.V. NETWORK VOYEURISM

86

PACK RATS

CARROT CAKE theatre

now playing:
"SOME BUNNY UP THERE
LIKES ME"

coming soon:
"EASTER RIDER"
"HOP GUN"
"PRETTY IN PINK NOSE"
"COTTONTAIL COMES TO HARLEM"
"MY LEFT RABBIT'S FOOT"
"BEVERLY HILLS HOP"
"UNCLE BUCKTOOTH"
"BUNNY AND CLYDE"
"EASTER WEEKEND AT BERNIE'S"
"BUNNY GIRL"
"THUMPER-BOLT AND LIGHTFOOT"
"THE FLOPPY EARS OF LAURA MARS"
"RABBIT FIRE"

©2010 Randy H

BUNNY PICTURES

88

FAN DANCERS

89

THE TURKEY VERSION of "RAMBO"

90

BUG BROADWAY, PART 2

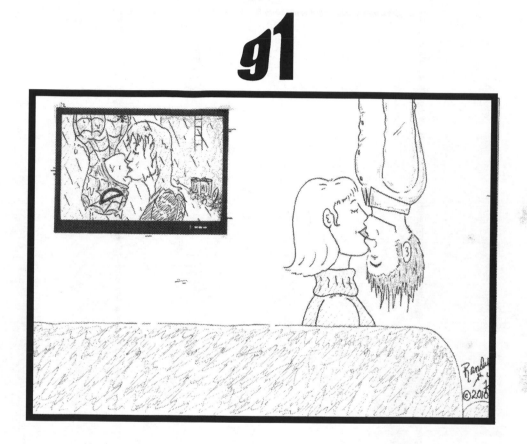

92

THE MAD, POSSESSIVE LIFE OF MISTER DIBS

GANGSTA RAP

95

NERD MOVIES

96

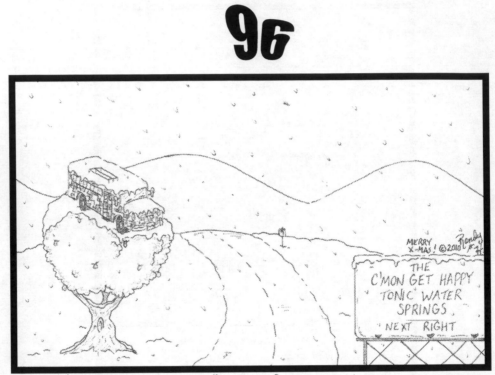

THE T.V. HOLIDAY CLASSIC "AND A PARTRIDGE FAMILY BUS IN A PEAR TREE"

BOOKS FOR OPTOMETRISTS

98

THE FIRST PARTY ANIMALS

99

Randy F H ©2010
The Wet Hen
VOL. 765
ISSUE 99
DEC. 6, 2010
MONDAY
CHICKEN WEEKLY
OBITUARIES
SCRATCHFOOT, 5 MONTHS
DECAPITATED FROM SHAVING WITH AXE
FEATHERHEAD, 6 MONTHS
BELOVED HEN DECAPITATED AFTER FALLING OFF BARN ROOF ONTO AXE
CLUCKY, 7½ MONTHS
COOP COMPANION FOUND DECAPITATED, COATED IN FLOUR, AND IN FRYING PAN
WINGNONA

FOWL PLAY

100

PHILADELPHIA TOURISM

101

102

THE INVISIBLE MAN MAKES A PRISON BREAK

103

IRRITABLE VOWEL SYNDROME

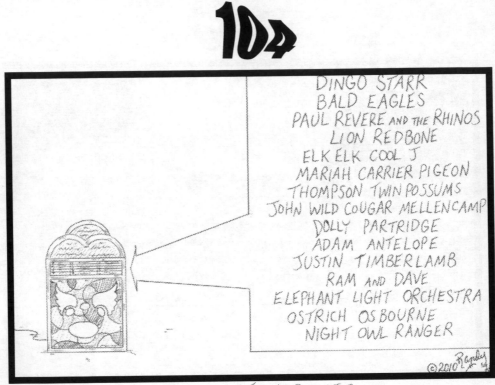

DINGO STARR
BALD EAGLES
PAUL REVERE AND THE RHINOS
LION REDBONE
ELK ELK COOL J
MARIAH CARRIER PIGEON
THOMPSON TWIN POSSUMS
JOHN WILD COUGAR MELLENCAMP
DOLLY PARTRIDGE
ADAM ANTELOPE
JUSTIN TIMBERLAMB
RAM AND DAVE
ELEPHANT LIGHT ORCHESTRA
OSTRICH OSBOURNE
NIGHT OWL RANGER

© 2010 Reynolds

ANIMAL JUKEBOXES

105

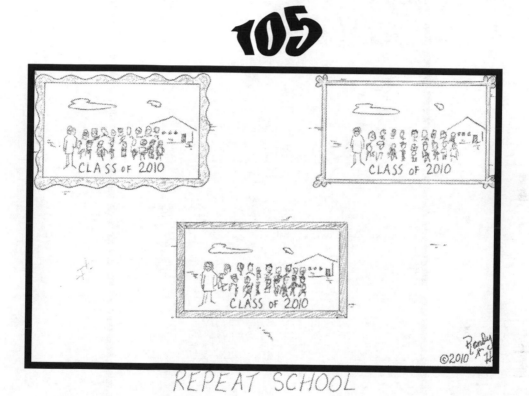

REPEAT SCHOOL

CAT FLICKS

THE FASHION POLICE

108

MEMORY FOAM MATTRESSES

109

FOGHAT COMES TO TOWN

112

ROCK 'EM SOCK 'EM ROBOT MARITAL SPATS

113

GRIM REAPER: THE COLLEGE YEARS

DIRTY CARPETS

DOESN'T PAY № 08 theatre

now playing:
"THE FELON AND THE SNOWMAN"
coming soon:
"LORD OF THE DRUG RINGS"
"ASSAULT AND BATTERIES NOT INCLUDED"
"FATHER OF THE BRIBE"
"ARSON AND OLD LACE"
"STEAL OF THE NIGHT"
"HOMICIDE ALONE"
"TERMS OF EMBEZZLEMENT"
"PLAY MISDEMEANOR FOR ME"
"PERJURY JACKSON AND THE OLYMPIANS"
"CAR JACK WASH"
"MENTALLY CRUEL INTENTIONS"
"MA AND PA KETTLE ON THE LAM"
"MOLESTATION FLANDERS"
"THE CRIME OF MISS JEAN BRODIE"
"THE BATTERED STEPFORD WIVES"

©2010 Randy Jr. H.

CRIME MOVIES

116

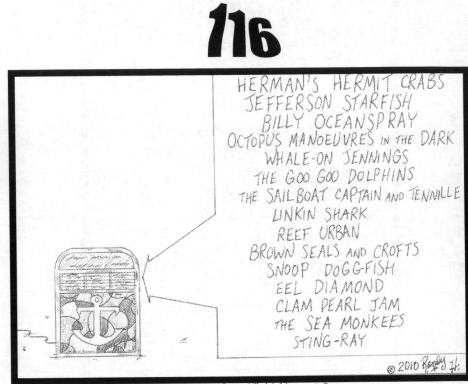

HERMAN'S HERMIT CRABS
JEFFERSON STARFISH
BILLY OCEANSPRAY
OCTOPUS MANOEUVRES IN THE DARK
WHALE-ON JENNINGS
THE GOO GOO DOLPHINS
THE SAILBOAT CAPTAIN AND TENNILLE
LINKIN SHARK
REEF URBAN
BROWN SEALS AND CROFTS
SNOOP DOGGFISH
EEL DIAMOND
CLAM PEARL JAM
THE SEA MONKEES
STING-RAY

© 2010 Rigby J.L.

SEA JUKEBOXES

117

SURGERY HUMOR

EXISTENTIAL INSURANCE SALESMEN

MY MOTHER, THE SLEIGH | RED & GREEN ACRES | ST
HAWAII FIVE-HO-HO-HO | THE JOLLY OFFICE | NOEL NEWS
EVERYBODY HATES KRIS KRINGLE | EVERYBODY LOVES REINDEER
ORNAMENT WINFREY | FIVE GOLDEN GIRL RINGS | X-MAS FILES
LOST PRESENTS | DESPERATE HOUSE-ELVES | CHIMNEY KIMMEL
REAL HOUSEWIVES OF NORTH POLE | SANTA NIGHT LIVE | BA
MOVIES: "CANDY CANE MUTINY" | "RIDING IN CARS WITH TOYS"
DOCUMENTARY: "THE CUBAN MISTLETOE CRISIS" | NEW

MERRY
X-MAS!

CHRISTMAS TELEVISION

122

TITANIC PRANKS

"HEADS UP!"

124

SCENE FROM "THE ROAD CONEHEADS"

125

NEARSIGHTED COP SHOWS

127

HEAD HISTORY

KHOW MEIN THEATRE

now playing:
"DESPERATELY SEEKING SUSHI"

coming soon:
"THE RICKSHAWSHANK REDEMPTION"
"CHEECH & CHONG'S RICE DREAMS"
"GEISHA, INTERRUPTED"
"PAINT YOUR DRAGON"
"THE CHINATOWN SYNDROME"
"BLACK BELT SWAN"
"THE TAKING OF PELHAM WONG-2-3"
"THE CHOPSTICKS AROUND THE CORNER"
"EGG FOO YOUNG GUNS"
"THE DEVIL WEARS A PRADA KIMONO"
"THE BROKEN FORTUNE COOKIE"
"SAW-KE"
"MIDNIGHT IN THE JAPANESE GARDEN OF GOOD AND EVIL"

©2010 Renks

ORIENTAL FLICKS

129

NEARSIGHTED COP SHOWS, PART 2

MRS. O'LEARY'S THEORY LEAVES THE
SCENE OF THE CRIME...

COWBOY TELEVISION

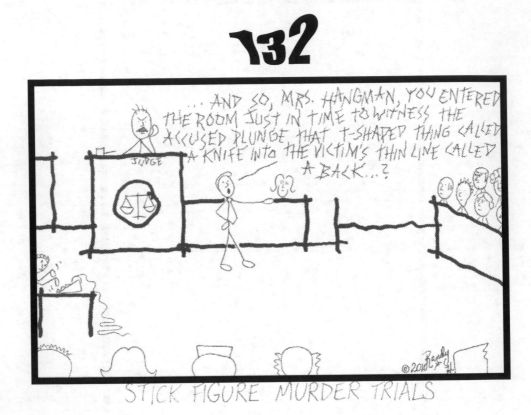

STICK FIGURE MURDER TRIALS

133

TRIVIAL HULK

134

136

"...THIS--SQUAWK!--MODEL HAS--BZZZT!--*ANY FEATURES, AND --BEEP!--*UST CAN'T BE BEAT ON-- ZAP!--*ERFECT RECEPTION...!"

137

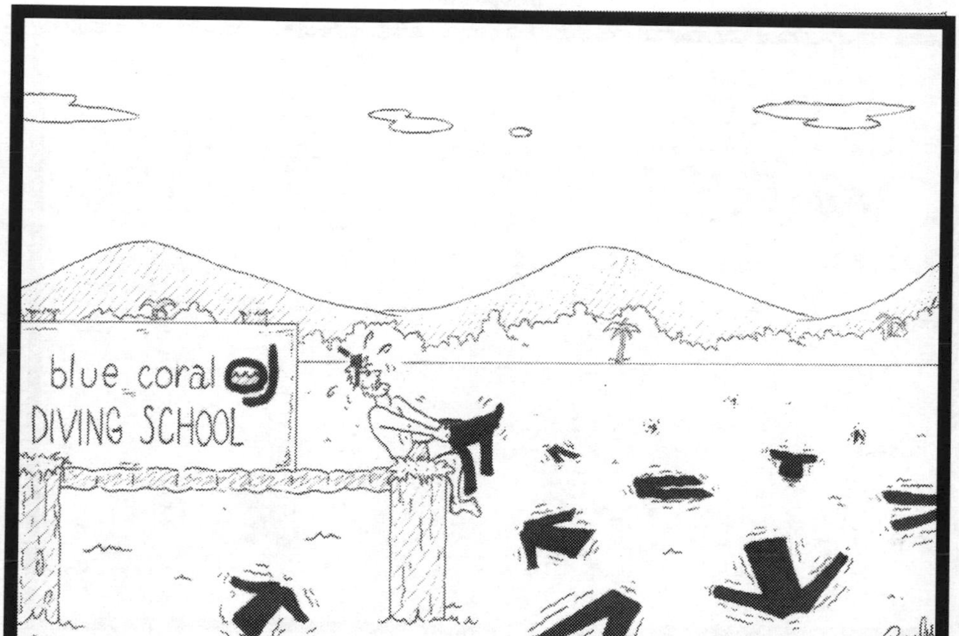

138

"WELL! HE'S CERTAINLY GOT HIS NERVE...!!"

Holidaze CINEMAS

now playing:

"THE PASSION of the CHRISTMAS"

coming soon:

"ANNIE HALL-OWEEN"

THE NEW YEAR of LIVING DANGEROUSLY

"EASTER of EDEN"

"THE FOURTH of JUNO"

"ST. PATRICK ELMO'S FIRE"

"GOODBYE, COLUMBUS DAY"

"FERRIS BUELLER'S PRESIDENT'S DAY OFF"

"THE VALENTINE'S HEARTBREAK KID"

"VETERAN'S DAY VERTIGO"

"LABOR DAY WEEKEND AT BERNIE'S"

"THANKSGIVING MY REGARDS TO BROAD STREET"

"SERIAL MOM'S DAY"

"THE COURTSHIP of EDDIE'S FATHER'S DAY"

©2011

HOLIDAY PICTURES

GHOUL COMEDY CLUBS

144

THE FILM CLASSIC "TOUGH GUYS IN 1940's PANTS"

145

GROSS BROADWAY

147

"...WE'VE TRIED COMPROMISE...WE'VE TRIED FINDING COMMON GROUND! BUT IT'S NO USE! WE JUST CAN'T SEE EYE TO EYE..."

148

THE OCTOPUS VERSION of "INDIANA JONES AND THE TEMPLE of DOOM"

149

LUCY ALWAYS YEARNED FOR VAMPIRE IMMORTALITY. BUT SHE SOON REGRETTED HER CHOICE OF THE COUNT FROM "SESAME STREET" TO DO THE DEED...

ELEPHANT MESSAGE BOARDS

151

152

T.V.'S CLASSIC POLICE DRAMA "ADAM-12"

153

ALTERNATIVE LIFESTYLE GUNS

154

GROSS BROADWAY, PART 2

154

156

TOWEL PSYCHIATRY

158

ALGAE GREEN
BACTERIA TURNER OVERDRIVE
FUNGI FOREIGNER
MICROBE AND THE MECHANICS
THE GERM GEILS BAND
THE ALAN PARASITE PROJECT
SOFT CELL NUCLEUS
AMOEBA FRANKLIN
COLLECTIVE SPORE
ARCHAEA ABBA
THEY MITE BE GIANTS
FLEETWOOD MOLD
GEORGE THOROUGHGOOD AND THE DECOMPOSERS
ALICE IN DNA CHAINS
DONNIE VIRUS

© 2011 Randy M. Sh.

MICROORGANISM JUKEBOXES

THE WEB MYSTERY "MURDER ON THE INTERNET EXPRESS"

DRAG MOVIES

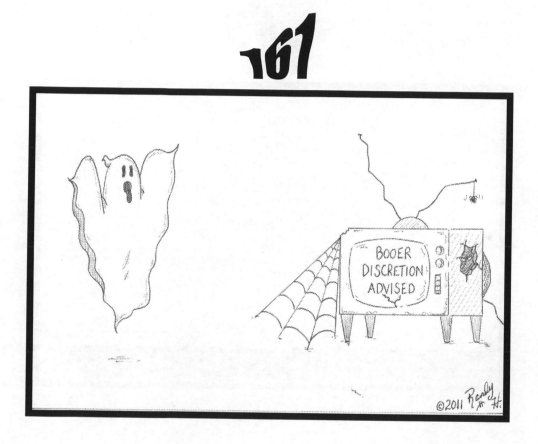

162

GROSS BROADWAY, PART 3

163

THE CHEEKY WESTERN "THE LOLLIPOP GANG IN TONGUE TOWN"

165

THE ALTERNATIVE TO THE "PSYCHO-KILLER-WITH-A-MEAT-HOOK"
CAMPFIRE STORY: "PSYCHO KILLER WITH A PROSTHETIC FINGER"

"NOT TO WORRY, MR. PORCUPINE! TURNS OUT YOU JUST HAVE
A BAD CASE OF PRICKLY HEAT!"

SHELVED FOR AN ETERNITY

SHALOM ✡ theatre

now playing:
"HANUKKAH MONTANA: THE MOVIE"

coming soon:
"THE WIZARD of OY"
"TWO YARMULKES FOR SISTER SARA"
"THE UNBEARABLE LIGHTNESS of BEING BAR MITZVAHED"
"YESHIVA, GIORGIO"
"LOCH, STOCK AND TWO SMOKING BAGELS"
"RABBI HOOD"
"SUMMER YENTL"
"A STAR of DAVID is BORN"
"STRANGE HEBREW"
"JEW'VE GOT MAIL"
"ROSH HASHANA HOUR"
"MENORAH IN BLACK"
"THE ACCOUNTANT of MONTE CRISTO"

©2011 Rawley

JEWISH PICTURES

IF CRITIC GENE SHALIT WERE AN OLD-TIME
MOVIE VILLAIN

BOOT CAMP

Beret cinemA

now playing:
"THE EIFFEL TOWERING INFERNO"

coming soon:
"THE GREAT ESCARGOT"
"MONSIEUR ROBERTS"
"SACREBLEU VELVET"
"MILLER'S CROISSANT"
"C'EST LA VIE ANYTHING"
"SOMEBODY UP THERE LIKES MOI"
"MILLION DOLLAR FROG LEGS"
"OUI MAN"
"CRÊPE EXPECTATIONS"
"WAITING... AT THE OUTDOOR CAFÉ"
"A SEINE RIVER RUNS THROUGH IT"
"PARIS BUELLER'S DAY OFF"
"MR. BLANDINGS BUILDS HIS DREAM CHATEAU"
"THE BONJOUR OF THE VANITIES"

©2011 Bentley

FRENCH FLICKS

GAME SHOWS FOR THE DENSE

BAD MERGERS

ROCK, PAPER, SCISSORS: an UNEASY ALLIANCE

CAT TELEVISION

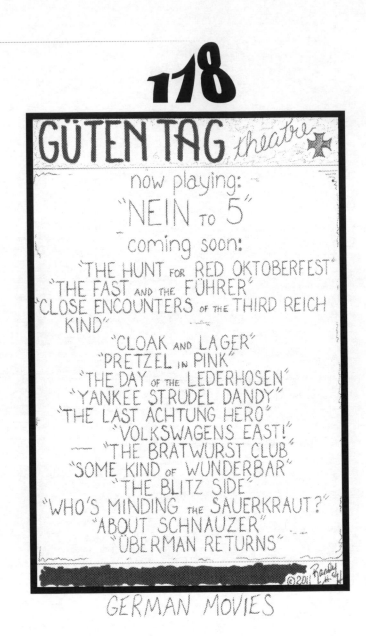

GÜTEN TAG *theatre*

now playing:
"NEIN to 5"
coming soon:
"THE HUNT for RED OKTOBERFEST"
"THE FAST and the FÜHRER"
"CLOSE ENCOUNTERS of the THIRD REICH
KIND"

"CLOAK and LAGER"
"PRETZEL in PINK"
"THE DAY of the LEDERHOSEN"
"YANKEE STRUDEL DANDY"
"THE LAST ACHTUNG HERO"
"VOLKSWAGENS EAST!"
"THE BRATWURST CLUB"
"SOME KIND of WUNDERBAR"
"THE BLITZ SIDE"
"WHO'S MINDING the SAUERKRAUT?"
"ABOUT SCHNAUZER"
"ÜBERMAN RETURNS"

© 2011 Randy

GERMAN MOVIES

179

OLD NEWS

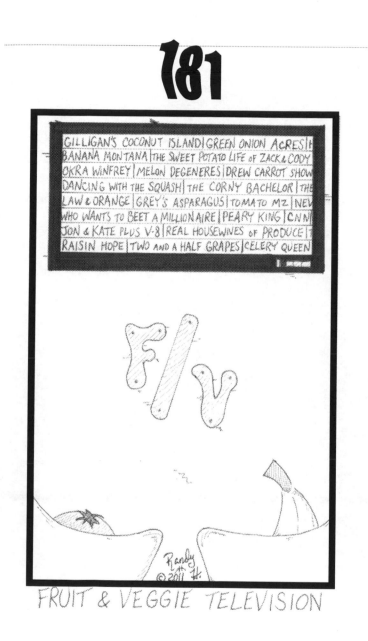

FRUIT & VEGGIE TELEVISION

182

SMALL APPLIANCE PARTIES

Moldy Movie Palace

now playing:
"CHEDDAR CHEDDAR
BANG BANG"
coming soon:
"SWISS ME KATE"
"AMERICAN CHEESE GRAFFITI"
"JAILHOUSE ROQUEFORT"
"THE BLUE CHEESE LAGOON"
"NACHO VILLA"
"MOZZARELLA ENCHANTED"
"SHE'S RICOTTA HAVE IT"
"MONTEREY JACKASS"
"COLBY MINER'S DAUGHTER"
"GORGONZOLAS IN THE MIST"
"AS GOUDA AS IT GETS"
"OUT ON A LIMBURGER"
"CURD ON A WIRE"
"BRIE IT ON"
"THE MEN WHO STARE AT GOAT'S CHEESE"

CHEESY PICTURES

MILITARY MOVIES

AUTHOR

Outside Haggin Museum in Stockton, CA

Photo courtesy of my niece, Shelby Rose
Foster. Thanks, Buggy!

Look for these other **Left Field** titles...

Which Way to Left Field?

Left Field, RELOADED

Left Field STRIKES BACK!

Left Field CONTROLS The UNIVERSE

Available at www.amazon.com!